Think
Exp
From The Inside Out

By
Gregory Dickow

Thinking Forward
Experience Change From the Inside Out

©2012 by Gregory Dickow Ministries.

All rights reserved.

No part of this book may be used or reproduced in any manner whatsoever—graphic, electronic, or mechanical—without written permission, except in the case of reprints in the context of reviews. Scripture quotations marked (AMP) are taken from the Amplified Bible, Copyright © 1954, 1958, 1962, 1964, 1965, 1987

by The Lockman Foundation. Used by permission.

Printed in the United States of America

For information, please write

*Gregory Dickow Ministries,
P.O. Box 7000
Chicago, IL 60680*

or visit us online at *www.gregorydickow.org*.

Table of Contents

Introduction 5
Day 1: I Feel Powerless 6
Day 2: I Can't 9
Day 3: I'm Afraid 11
Day 4: I Don't Feel Loved 14
Day 5: It's Too Late 16
Day 6: I've Messed Up Things Too Badly 19
Day 7: I Don't Have Enough 21
Day 8: Things Aren't Getting Better, They're Getting Worse . 24
Day 9: Backward Thinking 27
Day 10: I Feel So Angry 29
Day 11: I Feel Guilty. 31
Day 12: What's Wrong With Me. 34
Day 13: After What I've Done, I Don't Deserve To Be Blessed 37
Day 14: It's Hard To Find God's Will 39
Day 15: That's Just The Way I Am 41
Day 16: I Feel Unhappy A Lot 43
Day 17: I Feel Trapped 45
Day 18: The Devil Is More Powerful Than Me. 47
Day 19: I Could Succeed If I Had The Right Surroundings 49
Day 20: My Life Is Out Of Control. 52

Day 21: I'm Stuck.. 55
Day 22: Will I Ever Get Ahead 58
Day 23: I Can't Expect To Be Blessed All The Time 60
Day 24: I Can't Control My Emotions 62
Day 25: Don't Get Your Hopes Up 63
Day 26: Something Bad Is Going To Happen 66
Day 27: I'm Inferior....................................... 68
Day 28: I'm Running Out 70
Day 29: God Is Far From Me 72
Day 30: The Battle Is So Hard..................... 75
Day 31: Whatever Happens Must Be God's Will........ 77
Day 32: God Is Mad At Me 80
Day 33: If I Can Just Stop Sinning, I'll Be Holy and Pleasing To God.. 82
Day 34: I Just Can't Forgive Myself 84
Day 35: I'm So Depressed 87
Day 36: If I Just Find The Right Person, I'll Be Happy ... 89
Day 37: How Could I Ever Recover From This Loss..... 91
Day 38: Will God Do It 93
Day 39: I Can't Get The Victory 95
Day 40: It's Impossible............................. 97
Conclusion 99

Introduction

A Life-Changing Journey

I believe in effortless change! What I mean by that is: as we change the way we think on the inside, this leads to dramatic and revolutionary change on the outside. A number of years ago, I was frustrated with seeing so many people desiring to see change occur in their lives, but never seeing many results. Out of this frustration, I believe God spoke to me and said, "Call people to a 'fast from wrong thinking.'" In that moment, a movement was born, which has literally impacted hundreds of thousands of people around the world. It's a fast, not from food, but from wrong mindsets and thoughts that keep us limited and defeated. It's simply filling our minds with God's way of thinking, which amazingly, eliminates wrong ways of thinking. Quite simply, it's powerful. It's effortless. And it works.

The way we think controls our entire life. Our thoughts shape our actions; our actions shape our habits; our habits shape our character; and our character shapes our destiny. It all begins with our thoughts!

This devotional, **Thinking Forward: Experience Change From the Inside Out,** is a part of a uniquely-proven system of change that has helped people experience the victory in life that they have longed for.

You are about to experience a fresh SPIRITUAL REVOLUTION in your life by THINKING FORWARD! The Bible says in Philippians 3:13-14, "... *forgetting those things which are behind and reaching forward to those things which are ahead, I press toward the goal for the prize of the upward call of God in Christ Jesus.*" Well, "reaching forward" happens as we begin "Thinking Forward."

Proverbs 23:7 says, "As a man thinks within, so is he." Over the next 40 days, as you learn to control your thoughts, you will harness the power God has placed inside of you. Changing your thinking will release power, wisdom, healing, and give you a life of freedom and joy!

Let's begin Thinking Forward....

Day 1
"I FEEL POWERLESS."

As we launch a new chapter of our fast from wrong thinking, I'm asking the Lord to take you deeper into thinking patterns that will truly liberate you and establish a root system that will guarantee an abundant, fruitful life.

One of the greatest truths I have ever come to understand is that a "sense of powerlessness" is the root to all negative emotions. If you feel powerless to do anything about your past, you feel guilty. If you feel powerless to change your present condition, you feel depressed. If you feel powerless to change your future, you feel afraid. And when you feel like the people or circumstances of your life will not change, you feel angry.

Think about this for a moment: depression, fear, guilt and anger are four of the most powerful negative emotions you will ever experience. And ALL of them stem from a sense of powerlessness. The thought that there's not much we can do about the economy, our emotions, our weight, etc., imprisons us to a life of mediocrity and weakness.

We have all given into the thought that says, "I feel powerless."

LET'S CHANGE IT TODAY

1. **Embrace the truth** that God has not given you a spirit of fear, but POWER, LOVE and a SOUND MIND (2 Timothy 1:7). This is already done. You have this power in you.

2. **Believe that power is in you.** Ephesians 3:20 says, "God is able to do above and beyond all we can ask or think ACCORDING TO THE POWER that is at work within us." Be convinced—this power is in you now.

3. **Start thinking BIG & asking BIG. Give God something to work with.** Since He can do BEYOND what we ask or think, we have to at least give Him a base to begin with. We limit God when we don't think big and ASK big.

4. **Recognize and honor the Holy Spirit in you.** Acts 1:8 says, "You shall receive POWER when the Holy Spirit comes upon you..." Again, this power (the Greek word is dunamis=dynamite) is already in you. Thank God for the Holy Spirit in you. Romans 8:11 says, "The very *same Spirit* that raised Jesus from the dead lives in you."

5. **Take the limits off.** Don't limit God. Psalm 78:41-42 says that the children of Israel LIMITED God because they did not remember His power. We release our faith when we remember God's previous blessings in our lives. Psalm 103 says to not forget His benefits.

6. **EXPECT!** Never underestimate the power of expectation. Expect today for God's power to strengthen you; expect to be led by His Spirit today. We limit what God can do in our lives when we lower our expectations.

7. **Embrace your power:** the power to forgive and be forgiven (John 20:23); the power to heal (Mark 16:20); the power to speak the Word and get results (Job 22:28).

THINK IT & SAY IT

God has not given me a spirit of fear, but of power, love and a sound mind.

I have POWER in my life right now. Through the Holy Spirit in me, I have the power to overcome sin; the power to change my life for the better; the power to be healed; the power to forgive; the power to praise God no matter what; and the power to speak God's Word and see His promises show up in my life.

I will think big and ask big, and expect the POWER OF GOD'S SPIRIT WITHIN ME to bring it to pass in my life.

I choose to remember what God has already done, which takes the limits off of my life and my expectations. Today, I expect God's favor, wisdom, understanding, and blessing, in Jesus' Name

Day 2
"I CAN'T."

Today's thought that we are fasting from is simply: "I can't..."

There are so many things that we think we CAN'T do.

"I can't change. I can't believe that. I can't go on. I can't make it. I can't forgive. I can't recover. I can't get it done. I can't find a job. I can't find a spouse. I can't go back to college. I can't pay the bills. I can't figure this out." And the list could go on and on.

Believe me, this <u>MENTALITY</u> and <u>ATTITUDE</u>, sets us up to fail, to quit, and to live a negative existence. It is a poisonous thought that we must no longer eat or drink of.

From today on, we're replacing this thought with: "I can."

Philippians 4:13 declares, *"I CAN DO ALL THINGS THROUGH CHRIST WHICH STRENGTHENS ME."*

There's a saying that goes: "If you think you CAN or you think you CAN'T, you're right." Either way, you're right, because as a man thinks, so is he (Proverbs 23:7).

The Spirit of God lives in you. You CAN do what HE CAN do in you. 1 John 4:17 says, "As He is, so are we in this world."

LET'S CHANGE IT TODAY

1. **Remember the little engine that could!** Over fifty years ago, the book called, The Little Engine That Could, spoke to a generation of children: "I think I can. I think I can. I think I can," AND IT DID!

2. **Say it: "I can."** By simply saying this continually, your life will take the turn you desire.

3. **You ARE, therefore you CAN.** Remember that you ARE more than a conqueror, therefore you CAN conquer anything (Romans 8:37).
4. BELIEVE the Bible is written about YOU. **Fill your mind with Philippians 4:13:** "I can do all things through Christ which strengthens me!"
5. **Change your thinking. And change your habit.** GET the words "I can't" out of your vocabulary today. Stop yourself every time you feel like saying "I can't"; and let the new thought "I can" come out of your mouth. The more your ears hear your voice say this, the easier it becomes to believe it.

THINK IT & SAY IT

I declare I can do all things through Jesus Christ who strengthens me. I eliminate "can't" from my vocabulary. I can do anything God's Word says I can do. I submit my thinking to the Word of God and my whole life is changing today, in Jesus' Name.

Day 3
"I'm Afraid."

Today we're fasting from the granddaddy of all wrong thinking: *"I'm afraid."*

Fear is at the root of just about every negative thing that happens in our lives. We're afraid of failing, afraid of being alone, or rejected; afraid of running out of money; afraid that people will let us down; that we won't find a spouse or the one we found will leave us (or in some cases that they WON'T leave us—haha). We're afraid something bad may happen to us or our children, and the list goes on and on.

All fear is rooted in the core belief that God's Word won't work. For example, the fear of not having enough is rooted in the fear that Philippians 4:19 isn't true. If you believe that "God will supply all your needs according to His riches...", then fear leaves.

LET'S CHANGE IT TODAY

1. **Meditate on the fact that God's Word is true.** In John 17:17, Jesus said, "Thy Word is truth." What God says is fact—whether you feel it, see it, or whether you have ever experienced it.

2. **Consider God's track record.** 1 Kings 8:56 says, "…He has done all that He promised. Every word has come true of all His good promise…" (New Life Version). Fear leaves when you can rely on something that can't fail. God has never failed to fulfill His promises. There are over 1000 predictions or prophecies in the Bible—promises that God made before they happened. The chances of merely 17 of these coming to pass is ONE out of 450 billion x 1 billion x 1 trillion! Yet, not one of these 1000 promises have failed.

3. **Accept the truth that what we fear comes upon us.** In Job 3:25, Job feared that his children would curse God, and that's what happened. When you realize fear has the power to produce negative results, you stop dabbling in it. When a child learns what fire can do, he no longer plays with matches!

4. **Perfect love casts out fear** (1 John 4:18). Flood your mind with thoughts of love—God's love for you and what He was willing to do to rescue you. If He would die for you, while you were in sin, separated from God, there's just nothing He wouldn't do for you! Think on that, and fear will leave.

5. **There is a promise, from God's Word, for every need you will ever experience.** In fact, there are over 7000 promises in the Bible. That's 7000 solutions to life's problems! For example, there is a promise of protection in Psalm 91:1-12 which delivers you from the fear of evil, sickness or tragedy.

6. **Pause and dwell on the fact that God is with you.** Psalm 23:4 says, "Though I walk through the valley of the shadow of death, I will fear no evil—for YOU ARE WITH ME." God's presence is the secret to a fear-free life. All fear ultimately is a sense of God's absence, or our separation from God. By contrast, a sense of God's presence delivers us from fear. Hebrews 10:19 says we enter the holy place of His presence by the blood of Jesus. YOU ARE IN HIS PRESENCE NOW—therefore fear not!

THINK IT & SAY IT

God's Word is true whether I feel it or not. He has kept all of His promises and has never failed. Fear leaves me because I rely on something that can't fail—His promises.

What I fear comes upon me, therefore I will fear ONLY GOD, and He will come upon me! God loves me perfectly, and I will not think otherwise, no matter what!

God has made 7000 promises to me, because He knows I need them! God is with me, and therefore I will fear no evil.

God has not given me a spirit of fear, but of power, love and a sound mind, in Jesus' Name.

Day 4
"I Don't Feel Loved."

We have embarked upon the most significant journey of our lives—fasting from wrong thinking. And today's thought is probably the most important one any of us ever deal with. **Today, we are fasting from the thought that says, "I don't feel loved."** The number one need in every human life is to be loved. Yet sadly, so few actually enjoy a life where they continually feel loved.

LET'S CHANGE IT TODAY

1. **God's not mad AT you, He's mad ABOUT you!** Dispel the myth of an angry God. He poured out His wrath on Jesus while on the cross, so He could pour His love on you forever. God is Love (1 John 4:8).

2. **Our feelings follow our thoughts.** Flood your mind with the thought: "My Heavenly Father tenderly loves me!" (John 16:27 AMP)

3. **You and God are inseparable!** Nothing can separate you from the love of God (Romans 8:37-39). Believe this with every fiber in your being!

4. **Recognize your value.** The value of a piece of art is not determined by the cost to make it, but rather by HOW MUCH SOMEONE WOULD PAY TO HAVE IT. Similarly, your value is not determined by what you've done or not done. It's determined by how much someone would pay to ransom you. God paid with the blood of Jesus. That makes you as valuable to God, as Jesus Himself! You are priceless!

5. **Stop trying to earn something God has already given.** He loves you. Just BE LOVED. It can't be earned. It is a gift from God (John 3:16). Accept it.

6. **Reject THE VOICES OF REJECTION.** Look in the mirror and tell yourself that you are chosen by God, accepted and loved (Colossians 1:12, Ephesians1:6).

7. **Know your calling.** By this, I'm not referring to your calling to serve or to ministry or your profession. I'm talking about what God calls you. He calls you His ***beloved*** continually in the Bible. Do a word search. You are His ***beloved***. So, BE LOVED!

THINK IT & SAY IT

God is not mad at me, He's mad about me. His anger lasted for a moment, but His love & favor are for a lifetime! My heavenly Father tenderly loves me. God and I are inseparable. He continually calls me His beloved, therefore I will be loved by Him today. Nothing can separate me from His love. I am valuable and priceless to Him. I am as valuable to God as Jesus is. I receive His love by faith, in Jesus' Name!.

Day 5
"It's Too Late."

We are so "time conscious". We allow time to limit us and define for us what we're capable of or what God can do in our lives. **Today we're fasting from the thought that says, "It's too late."**

It's often ingrained in us that it's too late to change; too late to start a new career; too late to save your marriage; too late to recover from a terrible mistake; too late to start over again; or too late to be forgiven or have a second chance.

The truth is: IT'S NEVER TOO LATE!

When you realize that it's not too late, you have hope. You take action. You move forward. You stop thinking that it's futile and useless to do the right thing.

LET'S CHANGE IT TODAY

1. **UN-DECIDE that it's too late for these things to change.** Un-decide that you can't recover! Un-decide that the damage is irreversible. It's not too late to turn your finances around; to recover from a tragedy or mistake; to surrender your life to God; to take better care of yourself; to change the way you see yourself; to apologize; to break a bad habit; or to start saving.

2. **Meditate on the fact that God created time, and He can multiply it.** The earth and sun stood still in Joshua 10:12-13, which says, "And Joshua spoke to the Lord at Gibeon... and said in the sight of Israel, 'Sun, stand still at Gibeon, and moon in the valley of Aijalon'. So the sun stood still and the moon stopped." Joshua had control over time, for God's purpose. We need to start thinking that way - we have control over time. It doesn't control us!

3. **Think about the great cloud of witnesses**, for whom it wasn't too late:

- It wasn't too late for Abraham to be a father at 99 years old.
- It wasn't too late for Sarah to be a mother at 90!
- It wasn't too late for Peter after he denied the Lord 3 times.
- It wasn't too late for Paul after he had persecuted the church and killed other Christians! God later used him to write two-thirds of the New Testament after the book of Acts.
- It wasn't too late for the woman caught in adultery (John 8:1-11), the woman with the issue of blood (Mark 5:25-34), or the man who was lame at the pool of Bethesda for 38 years (John 5:1-10).
- In business, it wasn't too late for Ray Kroc, who at the age of 56 started the first McDonalds. (How did that work out for him?)

4. **Meditate on God's mercy and grace.** Lamentations 3:22-33 says, "His mercy is new every morning..." Hebrews 4:15 says, "Come boldly to the throne of grace to receive mercy and grace in your time of need." Mercy is when God doesn't give us the judgment that we DO deserve. And "grace" is when God gives us the goodness that we don't deserve.

5. **Adjust your thinking here: Stop making excuses for why it's too late.** God doesn't listen to our excuses. Realize, HE IGNORES OUR EXCUSES, and EXPECTS us to believe in His faithfulness. We claim we have low self-esteem or a disability. Moses wasn't confident and he had a speech impediment, but God gave him chance after chance to be used by Him to deliver God's people.

6. **Meditate on the verse in 2 Timothy 2:13:** "Even when we are faithless, He remains faithful. He cannot deny Himself."
7. **Ask God for more time and another chance.** Hezekiah did in 2 Kings 20:1-6. When Hezekiah turned back to the Lord, and asked for a second chance, God told him, "I have heard your prayer. I have seen your tears. Surely I will heal you...And I will add to your days FIFTEEN YEARS." If he did it for Hezekiah, He will do it for you!

THINK IT & SAY IT

I believe that it is not too late for things to improve in my life, and radically turn around.

I believe in the God of second chances. I can recover and there is nothing that God won't turn around in my life.

It is a fact that God created time and He can multiply it for me. I am not controlled by time. By God's grace, I control it!

It wasn't too late for Abraham or Sarah, Peter or Paul. It wasn't too late for the woman caught in adultery, and it's NOT TOO LATE FOR ME.

God is no respecter of persons, therefore if He multiplied time back for Joshua and Hezekiah, He will do it for me, in Jesus' Name!

Day 6
"I'VE MESSED THINGS UP TOO BADLY."

Today we're fasting from the thought that says, "I've messed things up too badly." "My mistakes are too great."

This thinking goes beyond feeling guilty. It reminds us of our failures—robbing us of creativity, initiative, and the power to live in God's fullness.

LET'S CHANGE IT TODAY

1. **Believe with every fiber of your heart and mind in the MERCY of God** (Hebrews 4:15-16). A woman asked Napoleon to have mercy on her son, who was about to be hanged. "Do you realize the crimes he's committed against France, madam? He doesn't deserve mercy," Napoleon answered. She responded, "If he deserved it, it wouldn't be mercy, Emperor." At that moment, her son was set free.

2. **Don't underestimate the power of confession** (1 John 1:9). Confessing our sins before God is both liberating and therapeutic. He is faithful to forgive, to cleanse and to heal (James 5:16).

3. **Do not allow your multiple mistakes to DEFINE you.** No matter how badly you've messed up, get up and live another day. You may have fallen, but you can and will get up! (Look up Proverbs 24:16)

4. **See the silver lining.** You HAVE become smarter. You ARE better. Your maturity and experience are going to show up in MORE important things ahead. Trust the work of God in you. Philippians 2:13 says, "God is at work in you, to will and work for His good pleasure."

5. **Think like a winner.** Romans 8:37 says you are more than a conqueror—no matter how far you've fallen, failed, or messed up, YOU ARE MORE THAN A CONQUEROR.

6. **Accept that God has not stopped loving you or believing in you.** Nothing can separate you from His Love (Romans 8:38-39). Nothing past, present or TO COME! You are not condemned.

THINK IT & SAY IT

There is now NO condemnation to me, because I am in Christ Jesus. I accept God's mercy in spite of all my mistakes. I will not allow my sins or failures to define me. I am the righteousness of God; therefore, no matter how far or how many times I've fallen, I can and will get up. He is at work in me still, and nothing shall separate me from His love—I am more than a conqueror, in Jesus' Name.

Day 7
"I Don't Have Enough."

Most people know the benefits of fasting from food, but 'fasting from wrong thinking' is unprecedented—until now. As you continue this amazing journey and tap into this power, you will arrive at a place of victory and peace in your life that you have never known before.

Victory or defeat in life is determined by what controls the decision making process of your life...and your decisions are determined by your thought life.

Today we are fasting from the thought that says: **"I don't have enough."**

This is a mindset, an attitude that says, "I don't have enough money. I don't have enough time. I don't have enough friends. I don't have enough experience. I don't have enough education..."

This thought is an invisible fence that keeps you in the backyard of lack and deficiency.

LET'S CHANGE IT TODAY

1. **Believe in God's abundant provision.** Our God calls Himself: El Shaddai - the God of more than enough! We have more than enough of God living inside of us—Romans 8:11. Let's stop thinking in terms of "not enough" and start thinking in terms of "more than enough."

2. **Think Multiplication.** God said be fruitful & multiply. He is a multiplier and so are you. Believe in the God of multiplication!

- In 1 Kings 17, there was more than enough for Elijah and the widow.
- In Exodus 16, there was more than enough for the children of Israel, everyday.
- In John 6, there was more than enough bread left over, after Jesus fed the 5000.
- In Mark 5, there was more than enough anointing to heal Jairus, the woman with the issue of blood, and all the people that were sitting by.

3. **Think: Apple Orchard.** An apple seed becomes an apple orchard. One little seed becomes more than enough apples for a whole community! Believe in the power of a seed.

4. **Seed meets need.** Remember, even God cannot multiply a seed that you don't sow. Sow a seed (Mark 4:26).

5. **Be patient.** Farmers understand there is seed, TIME, and harvest (Genesis 8:22). Don't forget that time is the connector between the seed and the harvest.

6. **God is not trying to get something FROM you. He's trying to get something TO you.** Trust. Let go. As you let go of what you have in your hand, God lets go of what He has in His hand. This is part of the great exchange. Give and it will be given back to you in good measure (Luke 6:38).

THINK IT & SAY IT

I always have enough, because Philippians 4:19 says God shall supply ALL my needs, according to His riches. I always have enough because My God is more than enough. I believe that seeds meet needs. I am a sower; and therefore I am a reaper. God is a multiplier and so am I. I am called to be fruitful & multiply. God is multiplying every good seed that I have ever sown. As I give, He gives back to me good measure, pressed down, shaken together and running over, in Jesus' Name!

Day 8
"THINGS AREN'T GETTING BETTER. THEY'RE GETTING WORSE!"

Today we're fasting from the thought that says, "Things aren't getting better. They're getting worse!"

Thinking this way is NOT AN OPTION.

This thinking keeps us bound to the past, or moving backwards. The media espouses negativity. The spirit of darkness is behind so many of the world's thoughts and mindsets. The devil promotes doom and gloom to get people depressed, on drugs, fearful and timid—distracted from the worship of God and the work of the gospel.

The world is full of bad news - the economy is getting worse, society is getting worse, etc. But we reject this thought TODAY!

LET'S CHANGE IT TODAY

1. **The path of the righteous...gets brighter and brighter until the full day** (Proverbs 4:18).

2. **"Evil men and impostors will go from bad to worse, deceiving and being deceived"** (2 Timothy 3:13). But the opposite is true about you! **Goodness follows you; therefore, you go from good to better!**

3. Adopt "running over" thinking. **Don't think "glass half full or glass half empty."** Think: My cup runs over (Psalm 23:5)!

4. **Your life is going to end up better than it started!** (Ecclesiastes 7:8 says, "Better is the end of a thing than the beginning.") Haggai 2:9 says, "The latter days of this house shall be greater than the former."

5. **Believe that God has saved the best for last.** John 2:10 says, "...But you have saved the best for last!" That's His nature. Your best days are ahead of you, not behind you.

6. **God only has the best in mind for you.** In Luke 15:22 the father said, "bring the best robe, and put it on my son..." We need to think like sons of God rather than slaves. We are not dogs waiting for the crumbs from the table. We are sons, and even when we've failed, God intends for us to experience His best!

7. **Follow the pattern of how God does things.** He takes us from the Old Covenant to the New Covenant; from the blood of animals to the blood of Jesus; from law to grace; from sin to righteousness; from sickness to health; from adversity to prosperity; from defeat to victory; from unclean to clean; and from empty to filled. Everything in God's kingdom gets better and better. The kingdom of God is in you (Luke 17:21) therefore, expect things to get better and better in every area of your life.

THINK IT & SAY IT

No matter what is happening in this world, things are getting better and better for me! God has made me righteous through His blood; therefore, my path is getting brighter and brighter every day.

My inner man is being renewed day by day. Evil people may go from bad to worse, but the goodness of God follows me, so I go from good to better, every day.

I can celebrate in the presence of my enemies, because my cup runs over and never runs out! God has saved the best for last in my life, and my latter days will be better than my former days, in Jesus' Name.

Day 9
"Backward Thinking"

Today, we're fasting from something that I call "backward thinking".

So often, we start our day, or our prayer with WHAT WE DON'T HAVE. Around the world today, people are focused on what they don't have and trying to figure out how to get it. This is what I mean by "backward thinking."

Anything good that is going to happen in our lives today, starts with getting our minds on what we ALREADY have, not what we don't have.

LET'S CHANGE IT TODAY

1. **THINK BACK, but not BACKWARD.** Every day, we need to THINK about the things God has already done. In Psalm 103:1-5, David said, "...forget none of His benefits—He pardons your sins, heals all your diseases, redeems your life from destruction, crowns you with lovingkindness and compassion..." Make a list—it will change how you look at your life.

2. **Focus on the 'prayer of thanksgiving'.** Start EVERY prayer thanking God for what He has already done for you (Philippians 4:6-7). This creates FAITH ENERGY. As you reflect on what God has specifically given you already, it awakens your ability to believe for more.

3. **Meditate on Philemon 1:6 which says,** "Your faith becomes effective, as you acknowledge every good thing already in you, through Christ Jesus." There is so much wealth inside you already. Discover it. Acknowledge it. Then you'll experience it!

4. **Step out of the comparison trap.** 2 Corinthians 10:12 says, "When we compare ourselves with one another, we misunderstand life." Confusion, misunderstanding, jealousy all set in when we measure ourselves with what others have or do.

   God has MORE THAN ENOUGH to go around for everyone. Don't compare and you won't despair.

5. **Develop selective memory.** Think back ONLY on the good that has happened in your life. FORGET the pain. Let go of the hurts and losses you've suffered. Philippians 3:13: forgetting what is behind....

6. **Believe in the God of Restoration. Expect God to make up to you the years that have been lost through your pains, mistakes and wrong ways of thinking.** In Joel 2:23-25, God said, "I will restore the years that have been devoured..."

THINK IT & SAY IT

I start my day with what God has already done in my life. I will bless the Lord at all times, His praise, shall continually be in my mouth. I am already complete in Jesus Christ. I think back only on the good God has done. I leave the pain of my past behind.

I give up comparing myself to others and believe that God has more than enough for me. I believe in the God of restoration and expect Him to make up to me all that I have lost through years of backward thinking, in Jesus' Name.

Day 10
"I Feel So Angry."

Today we are fasting from ANGER - thoughts like "I feel so angry" or "they make me so mad."

Anger is a powerful emotion that obviously can hurt ourselves and others. It leads to bad decisions, damaged relationships, stress and physical sickness. Let's conquer thoughts of anger today!

LET'S CHANGE IT TODAY

1. **Discover the power within you.** Remember, anger comes from a sense of powerlessness. When we feel powerless to change something, we get afraid, leading to anger. 2 Timothy 1:7 says God has not given us a spirit of fear, but POWER, love and a sound mind. Meditate on this verse. You have power.

2. **Listen quickly, speak slowly.** James 1:19 says be quick to hear, slow to speak, THEN the result: you will be slow to anger! Follow this simple pattern, and anger will lose its grip.

3. **Realize that anger does not work. It doesn't produce or achieve anything!** James 1:20 says, "For the anger of man does not ACHIEVE (WORK, PRODUCE) the righteousness of God." If you had an employee that didn't work, produce or achieve, you would fire them, right? FIRE your anger from your life, it doesn't achieve anything.

4. **Deal with unresolved conflict TODAY!** Ephesians 4:26 says, "Be angry, but do not sin. Do not let the sun go down on your wrath." Make peace with whomever

you have something against today (especially in marriage). Don't let it fester. You'll be amazed at how much less you feel angry.

5. **It's OK to feel it; but direct it the right way toward the devil.** Notice, the verse goes on to say, "Don't give the devil an opportunity to work." The devil wants you to blame others for why you're angry. But REALIZE, there's no one to blame but the slithering devil! And like a machine gun operator who just discovered the enemy, turn it completely on him; use your anger to resist the devil, speaking the Word with an aggressive force, and cut that old dragon to pieces!

6. **Get the whole picture.** So often, the reason we get mad or afraid is because we only see a snap-shot of what's really going on. As soon as anger comes, ask God to open your eyes to see the big picture. He did it for Elisha's servant (2 Kings 6:16-17). He will do it for you!

THINK IT & SAY IT

I am free from the power of anger. I have power over it. I have power, love and a sound mind. I will not act rashly, but choose to listen quickly and speak slowly.

I say to anger: YOU ARE FIRED! Since it doesn't work, achieve or produce for me, I will not continue to employ it. I resolve conflict today and will not go to bed angry.

I admit no one is to blame for my angry feelings. I will use what remains of my aggressive feelings against the devil, speaking the Word of God and resisting him FIRMLY in my faith. The violent take the kingdom by force, and that's what I'll do today, in Jesus Name.

Day 11
"I Feel Guilty."

Today, we're fasting from the thought that says: "I feel guilty."

We've all thought that or had thoughts that try to make us feel guilty such as: "You don't do enough. You're not good enough. You don't say the right things. You don't take care of yourself. You don't measure up. You don't do as much for others as you should. You eat too much, etc."

This line of thinking produces guilt, which leads to self-hatred, anger toward others, bad decisions, harsh words, procrastination and fear.

So often, we feel guilty because we THINK we don't do enough for God and for others. We often feel we are not good enough or holy enough.

This thinking has enslaved people for centuries. Nothing seems to rob us of our true purpose more than thoughts and feelings of guilt.

God doesn't motivate by guilt. That's manipulation. God motivates by love. Romans 2:4 says "It's the love and kindness of God that leads us to change."

Often people put a guilt trip on us, to get us to do something or to give in to them. God isn't like that, and He wants you free.

LET'S CHANGE IT TODAY

1. **Jesus declares you: NOT GUILTY.** This doesn't mean that you've never sinned or done wrong. This means that He washes all your sin & guilt with His blood. The Word of God declares Jesus as our "guilt offering," thus declaring us free from guilt.

2. **See what God sees.** Accept Colossians 1:22, which says through His blood "He presents you holy and faultless and unblameable in the Father's eyes." When God sees you, He sees Jesus—like when Jacob went before his father Isaac with the hair, skin & scent of his brother. The father saw Jacob as if he was Esau. And He sees you as if you were Jesus—without guilt.

3. **Meditate on Job 10:7.** "According to your knowledge, I AM INDEED NOT GUILTY..." (NASB) When a person is born-again, they are cleansed of sin and guilt by the blood of Jesus, and therefore: NOT GUILTY.

4. **When you blow it, don't deny it.** Admit it. Confess it. 1 John 1:9 says "If you confess your sin, He is faithful and just to forgive you and to CLEANSE YOU FROM ALL UNRIGHTEOUSNESS."

5. **It's already done!** Believe that it is already done! The last words of Jesus on the cross were: It is finished. At that moment, the price was paid for your sin and guilt. Hebrews 1:3 says "He cleansed us from our sin."

6. **Stop thinking that you have to FEEL GUILTY to be forgiven.** Sometimes we think we owe it to people to feel guilty and feel bad for everything. Stop thinking that. You don't owe anyone. Don't think guilt somehow pays for something. The blood of Jesus paid it all. When we feel like we owe God guilt or we owe it to others to wallow in guilt, it's an insult to His blood.

7. **Stop beating yourself up about what you haven't done.** We often punish ourselves with self-condemnation. We will never 'do enough' for God. That's why Jesus did it all. He paid for sin, the curse, and our failure. Our job is to BELIEVE.

8. **Rest in the fact that you don't have to be perfect.** God is not holding you to a perfect standard. Jesus is your perfection. JUST REST!

THINK IT & SAY IT

Jesus has declared me: NOT GUILTY. Even when I feel I don't do enough, or that I'm not good enough, God says FAITH IN HIM IS ENOUGH.

I don't have to feel guilty to be forgiven. I am forgiven by faith in Jesus. I receive God's forgiveness, since He already cleansed me from my sin. If I sin, I will admit it, receive His mercy and move on.

I stop, today, beating myself up about all that I haven't done, or have done. I choose to live in the now. I will enjoy the moment that I'm in and praise God in the midst of it.

I rest in the fact that He is my perfection. I don't have to be perfect. He already is, and I put my faith in Him, in Jesus' Name.

Day 12
"What's Wrong With Me?"

Our fast from wrong thinking is working. Stay on this journey with me. These seeds will produce the great harvests you have always wanted and needed in every area of your life.

Today we're fasting from the thought that says: "What's wrong with me?"

Have you ever thought that? Who hasn't? We have all had our bouts with sin-consciousness - a haunting awareness of all that we do wrong and all that is wrong about us.

The first problem with this thinking is: it is "me-centered" not "Jesus-centered." It's selfish. We are called to LOOK to Him—the Author and Finisher of our faith. In Hebrews 12:1, God says, "look up" not "look within."

It starts with developing a "righteousness consciousness" rather than a "sin consciousness".

The constant awareness of our "falling short" is where the devil and religion want to keep us. This keeps us defeated and hemmed in by our human nature, rather than liberated through our divine nature. 2 Peter 1:4 says, "Through His promises, we share in the divine nature of God and escape the corruption that is in the world through lust."

LET'S CHANGE IT TODAY

1. **Understand the gift of righteousness.** 2 Corinthians 5:21 says, "He who knew NO sin, was made to be sin FOR US, that we would be MADE the righteousness of God." This is the greatest EXCHANGE in human history! Jesus took

our sinfulness and imparted to us His righteousness—which means we are RIGHT in God's eyes, not wrong. We are justified. I like the play on words here. Justified = "just if I'd" never sinned.

2. **Awake to righteousness.** 1 Corinthians 15:34 (Amp.) says, "Awaken to righteousness; and you will not sin." You are a child of God. You are forgiven. You are a joint heir with Jesus Christ (Romans 8:16). When God looks at you, He sees the blood He shed. He sees His Son. When God thinks of you, He thinks of a victorious, conquering, strong, powerful, wise, and holy son or daughter. He sees you as a mighty champion. The head and not the tail (Deuteronomy 28:13).

Righteousness means: to stand in the presence of God as if sin had never been. To stand in His presence without a sense of guilt, shame, inferiority or condemnation.

3. **Reject sin-consciousness.** When you are always conscious of what's wrong, you will DO wrong. When you are always conscious of BEING the righteousness of God - you will DO right. You'll act on the outside how you see yourself on the inside. (Whenever you think of your "wrongs", cast them upon Jesus. And remember, His "rights" are now yours!)

4. **Ask the Holy Spirit to do what He does best.** 1 Corinthians 2:12 says, "....we have received the Spirit of God, so that we may know the things freely given to us by God." A key ministry of the Holy Spirit is to REVEAL what is already yours (NOT TO REVEAL TO YOU ALL THAT IS WRONG IN YOUR LIFE).

5. **Dwell on what's right rather than what's wrong.** Go through the Scripture regarding who you are in Christ; what is yours in Christ, and what you can do in Christ. It's staggering. Flood your mind with this new way of thinking.

THINK IT & SAY IT

I decide to give up thinking about all that is wrong in my life, and I choose to think about what is right.

I am the righteousness of God, through the blood of Jesus. I stand in the presence of God without guilt, shame, inferiority or condemnation.

I awake to righteousness and believe it will lead me to a victorious life.

I am a joint heir with Jesus. When God looks at me, He sees His blood. He thinks of me as a conquering, powerful and holy son or daughter. I will not think of myself as anything less or more than what God thinks of me in Jesus Name!

Day 13
"After What I've Done Wrong, I Don't Deserve To Be Blessed."

Today, we're fasting from the thought that says: "After what I've done wrong, I don't deserve to be blessed."

LET'S CHANGE IT TODAY

1. **Stop focusing on your "wrongs," and focus on His "rights".** We've all done enough wrong in life to send us straight to hell. But God doesn't judge us based on our right or wrong. He judges us based on what Jesus did right. We need to believe it.

2. **It's His choice. The first thing God did when He created man was: He blessed them. That's His choice because that's His nature.** Accept that. Embrace it. God has appointed you to be fruitful and blessed (John 15:16).

3. **Blessing flows when you believe you are forgiven.** Romans 4:7 says, "Blessed are they whose sins are forgiven." This is amazing! Putting your faith in God's forgiveness is the gateway to blessing in your life.

4. **Jesus deserves to be blessed.** And since He's worthy of God's blessing, that makes you worthy to be blessed, IN HIM. 1 John 4:17 "...as He is, so are we in this life."

5. **Stop condemning yourself. STOP BEATING YOURSELF UP WHEN YOU MAKE A MISTAKE.** Romans 14:22 says, "Blessed & happy is the man who does not condemn himself."

6. Jesus took the curse so you could take the blessing! Jesus deserves to see you blessed, because of what He went through to redeem you from the curse! "Christ redeemed us from the curse of the law, having become a curse for us... on the cross...that the blessing of Abraham might come on us through Jesus Christ" (Galatians 3:13).

THINK IT & SAY IT

I take my eyes off all that I have done wrong, and put my eyes on all that He has done right for me. He blesses me, because He has chosen to. I receive it. I choose to believe I am forgiven, and therefore BLESSING FLOWS. I belong to Christ; therefore, I am blessed with Abraham. Genesis 24:1 says Abraham was blessed IN ALL THINGS - therefore that's what I expect, in Jesus' Name.

Day 14
"It's Too Hard To Find God's Will."

Today we're fasting from the thought that says: "The will of God is such a mystery." Or, "It's too hard to find God's will."

Many people struggle so hard to do the will of God, only to be frustrated, and often confused. Can we ever be SURE of the will of God? We can. And I believe this will help.

1. **Change the way you look at the Bible.** We need to look at the Bible as a love letter, a description of who we are in Christ, and a collection of divine seeds for the harvests of life.

2. **Today, you must see the Bible as a "Will".** It is God's LAST WILL & TESTAMENT (Hebrews 9:15-17). Enclosed in the Bible is EVERYTHING Jesus, after dying, has left to His loved ones—that's you and me!

3. **Remember, a will goes into effect when someone dies.** Hebrews 9:17 says, "because a will is in force only when somebody has died; it never takes effect while the one who made it is living."

4. **See yourself in God's will NOW.** Through Jesus' blood and His death, God has placed us IN His will.

5. **The gospel is: forgiveness AND an inheritance that now belongs to us (Acts 26:18).** Read the Scriptures to discover your inheritance, and know what belongs to you NOW.

6. **Now, take the pressure off yourself in trying to discover what to DO, and focus on discovering what is YOURS.**

This will change how you look at yourself and how you live!

7. **Don't try to find the will of God. It will find you.** Just meditate on God's Word. Flood your mind with His promises. Bask in His love & grace and the will of God will find you. It will overtake you (Deuteronomy 28:2).

THINK IT & SAY IT

God has placed me in His will. I don't have to strive to find it. God's will is His covenant toward me—His promised inheritance is mine through the blood of Jesus. I will see the Bible as God's will TOWARD me. I will read it to discover what belongs to me and who I truly am in Him, and the will of God will track me down. It will come upon me and overtake me, in Jesus' Name.

Day 15

"That's Just The Way I Am."

Today we are fasting from the thought that says: "That's just the way I am."

One of the things that limits us and keeps us defeated is the opinion we have of ourselves. Over time, we begin to accept that we can't change. We also accept other people's stigmas of us. These things begin to shape our view of ourselves and what we're capable of.

"He's shy." "She's stuck up." "He's all talk." "She's not the sharpest knife in the drawer."

We often end up living up to the very opinions and expectations that others have had of us, because it has conditioned us. Or we feel, "I'll always be average." "I'll always be overweight." "I'm capable of only making 'x' amount of money." We're limited by our self-imposed expectations of ourselves.

Today, we are breaking out of the limitations and boundaries we, or others, have put on us. That may have been the way you were, but that's not the way you are.

LET'S CHANGE IT TODAY

1. **You are a work of art—a work in progress.** God is the potter and we are the clay (Jeremiah 18:1-6). God is working on you to make you what He wants you to be. Trust the Artist to make a masterpiece. Be flexible and adaptable. See yourself as a GOOD work in progress.

2. **Withhold judgment of yourself (or others).** Philippians 1:6 says, "He who began a GOOD work in you will complete it until the day of Jesus Christ." Don't pre-judge what your capacity is or what your potential is. He's only just begun!

3. **God doesn't throw you out.** HE NEVER GIVES UP ON YOU. Jeremiah 18:4 says, "the clay was marred, so He made it again." He didn't discard it. He made it again. Whew! Thank God!

4. **You are changing as you are reading this!** Whatever flaws you have, they are not the final sentence. You are NOW being conformed to the image of Jesus (Romans 8:29)!

5. **EMBRACE the GRACE!** Paul said in 1 Corinthians 15:10, "I AM what I AM by the grace of God." It's God's grace IN YOU that is making you what you are. You are not a composite of your parents' mistakes, your mistakes, and others' opinions of you. You're awesome!

THINK IT & SAY IT

I am unlimited in my ability to grow and change. God is the potter and I am the clay. I am what God says I am. He began a good work in me, and He will finish it. He is making me into something GOOD.

I am His workmanship—His work of art. He's good at this and has been doing it a long time! I am not in bondage to my weaknesses and former limitations. They do not define me.

Every day and every moment that passes is making me more and more like Him, in Jesus Name!

Day 16
"I Feel Unhappy A Lot."

Today we're fasting from the thought that says, "I feel unhappy a lot."

LET'S CHANGE IT TODAY

1. **Happiness was God's idea!** Psalm 144:15 says happy are the people whose God is the Lord. When Jesus became the Lord of your life, a supernatural force of happiness was deposited in you! Make a withdrawal on the deposit by declaring: "Jesus is Lord and that makes me happy!"

2. **Reject the mindset that others need to treat you right in order for you to be happy.** Trust God = Happiness. (Proverbs 16:20). We hang on to what people will do for us or say about us, in hopes that it will make us happy. Give that up today.

3. **Take control of your life!** When you depend on someone else to act a certain way or treat you a certain way, you give up the control and power of your life over to them. Take it back.

4. **Let go of condemnation.** Romans 14:22 says, "Happy is the one who does not condemn himself…" Romans 8:1 tells us there is no condemnation for those in Christ. When you accept that God does not condemn you, you will discover the power to be happy and free!

5. **The supreme happiness in life is the ASSURANCE that you are LOVED.** BE LOVED. The Father tenderly loves you (John 16:27)!

6. **Jesus was the HAPPIEST man in the world** (Hebrews 1:9). Change your view of your Savior. He was a man of grief ONLY ON THE CROSS. In His daily life, He rejoiced more than anyone. And He lives in you (Colossians 1:27).

7. **You are in His presence NOW.** Remember that in His presence is fullness of joy (Psalm 16:11). And you are in His presence by the blood of Jesus (Hebrews 10:19).

THINK IT & SAY IT

I reject the thought that anyone can make or break my happiness. I take back control of my life, and I choose to be happy today, because Jesus is my Lord. I have a rich deposit of joy inside of me. And I release its force every time I open my mouth with praise. The ultimate happiness in life is the assurance that I am loved. And since God loves me, I walk in the supreme happiness of life. I am free from condemnation because the happiest Man in the world, lives in me, in Jesus' Name!

Day 17
"I Feel Trapped."

Today we're fasting from the thought that says, "I feel trapped."

Ever felt like that? We all know what it feels like when it seems we have nowhere to turn. Perhaps you've felt like life was closing in on you—like there was no way out of the situation you're in. Perhaps you feel bombarded by your daily responsibilities and you feel in bondage to your weaknesses and fears.

LET'S CHANGE IT TODAY

1. **God ALWAYS provides a way of escape** (1 Corinthians 10:13). When you feel trapped or closed in, God will make a way for you. He always does. Choose to believe it today.

2. **Expect an open door.** He opens the door that no one can close (Revelation 3:8). This is the favor of God. Psalm 5:12 says that His favor surrounds you like a shield. When you feel surrounded by your problems, declare that you are surrounded by HIS FAVOR!

3. **You have the wisdom of God.** Be confident of this. You will instinctively know what to do next. When you feel trapped, wisdom will open a door or create a door that wasn't even there before! 1 Corinthians 1:30 says Jesus has been made unto you wisdom from God.

4. **Change your perspective.** When Paul was trapped, despairing even of life, in 2 Corinthians 1:8-10 (Message translation), he said IT WAS THE BEST THING THAT COULD HAVE HAPPENED because he was forced to trust God totally. TRUST HIM TOTALLY TODAY.

5. **Stop thinking about the finish line.** Keep walking by faith. Just take one step in the right direction. God will meet you there. John 5:8—just start. Get up. You don't have to figure it all out. One step at a time.

6. **You have the peace of God in you.** When everything is closing in on you, declare, "Peace, be still." This is why Jesus could calm the storm with "PEACE". Because the peace was already in Him. And therefore, it's already in you!

7. **Embrace the thought:** "God will deliver whoever calls on His name" (Romans 10:13). He is your deliver. When you feel trapped, yell: JESUS, You are my Deliverer!

THINK IT & SAY IT

God makes a way where there is no way. There is always a way out of feeling trapped. I have the wisdom of God, and I walk by faith, not by sight. I speak to my situation, "Peace, be still." I expect God to open a door that no man can close. No matter how trapped I feel, I will totally trust God. And He will deliver me, as I call upon the Name of Jesus, in Jesus' Name!

Day 18
"The Devil Is More Poerful Than Me."

Today we're fasting from the thought that says, "The devil is more powerful than me." Many people give the devil far more credit than he is due, and they often over-estimate his power. I am not saying that he doesn't operate in powers of deception; however we are not under his authority. We are directly under the Lord's authority. We must attack this mindset that "the devil is more powerful than us."

LET'S CHANGE IT TODAY

1. **The devil has ALREADY been defeated at the cross of Jesus Christ!** (John 19:30) When Jesus said, "It is finished", He paid the price for the sin and the curse. When He rose from the dead, He conquered death and the devil. We are not still fighting the devil. Jesus defeated him.

2. **Spiritual warfare is: the fight of faith. It's not the fight over the devil.** Jesus destroyed the works of the devill (1 John 3:8). Our battle is to believe. As we resist the devil by being firm in our faith, we enforce the victory that Jesus won.

3. **In every situation, think: It is written!** Another way we enforce Jesus' victory over the devil is by speaking God's Word (Matthew 4:4)! As we do, devils tremble and Satan flees.

4. **Let your head CATCH up to your heart!** Though God has made us righteous in our heart by the blood of Jesus, we need to convince our heads of this truth (1 Corinthians 15:34, Romans 5:17).

5. **TAKE YOUR SEAT!** You have been SEATED with Christ FAR ABOVE all the power of the enemy (Ephesians 2:6, Ephesians 1:21).

6. **In Christ, you are just like Jesus!** 1 John 4:17 says, "As He is, so are we in this life!" His victory is your victory. We rule and reign with Him (Romans 5:17, 8:16-17).

THINK IT & SAY IT

The devil IS ALREADY DEFEATED. I walk by faith in the victory that is already mine. I am seated with Christ FAR ABOVE all the power of the enemy. As Jesus is, so am I, in this world. I accept the royalty that He paid for me to have, and I rule and reign with Jesus over life, in Jesus' Name!

Day 19
"I Could Succeed If I Had The Right Surroundings."

Today we are fasting from the thought: "I could succeed if I had the right surroundings, the right people or the right breaks."

So many people believe that if their surroundings were better, they would succeed. If they just moved to a different city or had a better boss or if someone gave them a chance, they would prosper. They use these thoughts as excuses for why things don't get better or why they don't reach their goals and improve their lives. This way of thinking leads to blaming others and circumstances for why things don't get better.

LET'S CHANGE IT TODAY

1. **It's not what surrounds you, but what's inside you that causes success!** 2 Corinthians 4:16 says, "Therefore, we do not lose heart. For though our outer man is decaying, yet our inner man is being renewed day by day." Notice, Paul is saying, even when things go the opposite direction on the outside, something good can be happening on the inside.

   When things go wrong on the outside, deal with the inside! This is the key to success. And what does God say we should do on the inside? Be renewed day by day. Be filled with the Word day by day! Absorb these Scriptures day by day, and the INSIDE will OVERTAKE the OUTSIDE!

2. **Success or failure in life is created by how you think.** Never forget our foundational verse in Proverbs 23:7: As a man THINKS, so is he. And Joshua 1:8 says "...but you shall meditate on the Word of God day and night...for THEN you shall make your way prosperous and THEN you shall have good SUCCESS."

3. **Understand the source of blessing.** Psalm 1:1-3 says, "Blessed is the man that ... meditates on the Word day and night. He will be like a tree firmly planted by streams of water, whose leaf does not wither, who bears fruit in his season, and whatever he does, prospers!"

4. **The root to true success is a prosperous soul.** 3 John 2 says, "Beloved I wish above all things that you would prosper and be in health, EVEN AS your soul prospers."

5. **Remember Joseph...thrown into a pit by his brothers and sold into slavery.** Genesis 39:2 says, "But the Lord was with Joseph, and so he became a successful man." Notice, even though his surroundings were terrible, HE STILL BECAME A SUCCESSFUL MAN. He had bad surroundings, bad breaks, was surrounded by bad people, and yet still succeeded BECAUSE GOD WAS WITH HIM.

6. **We affect our surroundings and we create our breaks by the thoughts we think and the choices we make.** Deuteronomy 30:15,19 says, "I have set before you life and prosperity; or death and adversity...Choose life!"

THINK IT & SAY IT

It's not what surrounds me that determines my success. It's what's inside me.

I will not lose heart. Even when things go wrong on the outside, I am being renewed on the inside by the Word of God, which will bring success in every area of my life.

My success is created by how I think. I agree with God's

thoughts and meditate on God's Word day and night. Success follows me. I prosper in my soul. I fill my mind with the richness of God's Word, and therefore it spills over into every area of my life.

Like Joseph, I will not allow my negative circumstances to determine my success or failure. <u>I AM A SUCCESSFUL</u> and <u>PROSPEROUS MAN OR WOMAN</u>, because God is with me, in Jesus' Name!

Day 20
"My Life Is Out Of Control."

Today we are fasting from the thought that says: "My life is out of control!"

That's what the devil wants you to think. He wants you to feel helpless and "under" the circumstances. When you think this way, you get discouraged. You lose hope. You give into things. Like a jellyfish, you are carried by the prevailing current.

LET'S CHANGE IT TODAY

1. **Think above.** Stop for a moment and understand what I'm saying here. Think "above". Think from a higher point of view. Look down at life rather than "up" at it. When Elisha's servant saw from "above", he realized there were more for him than those against him (2 Kings 6:14-17). Notice, God didn't add any chariots. They were always there. Elisha's servant just couldn't see them, because he wasn't thinking "above." THINK ABOVE.

2. **DON'T see the bigger picture today.** That's not a typo! Think of your situation and your world as small. Think of yourself bigger. Don't forget—how YOU see yourself, is how life will see you. That's how the devil will see you. That's how your mountain will see you. If you see yourself bigger than the mountain (Greater is He that is in you—that makes you big!), then the mountain will respect what you say when you tell it to move!

3. **The best day of your life is the day you decide your choices are your own; therefore, your life is your own.** No excuses. No one to blame. Remember the lame man at the pool of Bethesda for 38 years? He stayed in his condition because he told Jesus what he had believed for all those years: "I have no one to help me" (John 5:7). DECIDE TO OWN YOUR CHOICES and you will own the life God wants you to have.

4. **Focus on the inside, not the outside.** If you're like me, there are several things on the outside that are not fully under control, but that's not your job. Your job is to get control of the inside. That's what this fast from wrong thinking is about. It's taking care of the INSIDE. You ARE in control, IF you control your thought life.

5. **Take control of your day, one thought at a time.** Don't be overwhelmed. Isaiah 28:13 says that we build God's Word and God's thoughts in our lives: "line upon line, precept upon precept."

THINK IT & SAY IT

I am in control of my life, because I am in control of my thoughts. I rule my life by ruling my thoughts. My thoughts liberate my emotions, my health, my relationships and my whole life.

I think ABOVE beginning today. I choose to look down at life, rather than look up at it. I see it from God's point of view. I'm bigger than my problem, bigger than the mountain, bigger than any enemy I face today.

Greater, larger and more dominant is HE that is in me, than he that is in the world. TODAY IS THE BEST DAY OF MY LIFE, because I have control of the choices I make.

I will not stay in a defeated, lonely, sick, depressed condition another day of my life. I focus on the inside. I know the thoughts of victory that I am developing will take care of my outside. This fast from wrong thinking is working IN ME, in Jesus' Name.

Day 21
"There's Nothing I Can Do About My Situation."

Today, we are fasting from the thought that says: "I'm stuck." "There's nothing I can do about my situation. There's just no way."

We've all thought that at times. Sometimes we feel we've blown it, or we're at the end of our rope. There's nothing we can do. But it's a lie. There's always something that we can do. There's always a way.

The devil would love for you to believe there's nothing you can do about your situation. He wants you stuck! He wants you immobilized. He wants you defeated. And he achieves that by getting us to believe this lie.

This way of thinking keeps you from being decisive and taking action. Action produces results. But the thought that you can't do anything about your situation, or you don't know what to do about it, STOPS ACTION.

LET'S CHANGE IT TODAY

1. **Believe in the ministry of the Holy Spirit in your every day life.** Romans 8:26 says, "We don't always know how to pray as we should, but the Spirit intercedes for us..." No matter what your situation is, the Holy Spirit knows how to bring about God's will for your life, as you pray and worship Him.

2. **Think this thought today: PRAYER CHANGES THINGS.** There's nothing you can't impact with prayer. Prayer gets you unstuck. It gets you moving again toward victory. Prayer is powerful. "And all things, whatsoever you shall ASK in prayer, believing, you SHALL RECEIVE" (Matthew 21:22).

3. **Believe that FAITH FINDS A WAY.** In Mark 2:1-5, the friends of the paralyzed man could not find a way into the house where Jesus was. They were stuck. BUT THEY BELIEVED THERE WAS SOMETHING THEY COULD DO ABOUT THE SITUATION. By believing there was a way, they found one! They went up on the roof and lowered him down through the ceiling tiles, and the man was healed. Why? Because faith found a way! When we don't think it, we don't look for it.

4. **Remember, Jesus is the 4th man in the fire.** When it seemed like the three Hebrew men were going to be burned in the fiery furnace, Jesus showed up. What was an impossible situation was made possible, because Jesus was with them. AND HE IS WITH YOU in your fire.

5. **Jesus is your WAY.** John 14:6 says, "I am the WAY, the truth and the life." He is "the way" when there just seems to be no way. He IS YOUR WAY out of whatever situation you are in. EXPECT HIM to make a way.

6. **Just think: Next step. You don't have to figure it all out right away.** When you feel stuck, just take one step forward. When Jesus was tempted to back down, and not go to the cross – the Bible says, "He went forward a little..." (Mark 14:35). When you feel paralyzed—like there's nothing you can do—just take a step. Don't think about all the steps. Just take the first one. In a relationship, the first step may be saying you're sorry. If it's finances, maybe it's just cutting one area of spending, or giving one extra offering. If it's in your health, take the first step and have a salad. Just take that one little step!

THINK IT & SAY IT

I believe the Holy Spirit is interceding for me when things aren't working out. He will work through the situation to bring about God's will. He will bring me through.

As I pray, I believe things will change; they will improve. I walk by faith, not by sight, and faith finds a way.

I THINK AND BELIEVE THERE IS ALWAYS A WAY, even when it seems like there is none. And that way of thinking opens doors for me. Jesus is the Way when there is no way.

He is with me no matter what fire I'm in and no matter what the situation. I expect Him to make a way for me.

When I feel stuck, I will think about one step I can take that will move me toward healing, toward blessing, and toward God's will for my life, in Jesus' Name.

Day 22
"Will I Ever Get Ahead?"

TODAY we are fasting from the thought that says, "Will I ever get ahead?"

Real progress and success start in our thinking. A Washington Post survey revealed 4 out of 5 middle class Americans say they CAN'T get ahead. This has to change. Aren't you tired of just "getting by"?

LET'S CHANGE IT TODAY

1. **Believe in the abundant life Jesus came to give you.** In John 10:10, Jesus said, "...but I have come that you would have life in abundance, to the full, till it overflows!" God has called you to thrive, not just survive.

2. **No excuses here!** If you look for an excuse, you'll find one. But if you look for a way to make progress, the way will open. Luke 5:19 says "...not finding any way, they went up on the roof." If we keep looking for a way to get ahead, we will find it.

3. **YOU ARE THE HEAD!** Therefore you will GET ahead. Fill your mind with what God made you. Whatever you ARE inside is WHERE you will GO on the outside. God says about you, "You are the head and not the tail..." (Deuteronomy 28:13). Your life follows what you are focused on. It is a natural process. What you see is what you'll be!

4. **You control your economy.** God says we reap what we sow. Don't give into the lie that you are a product of the economy. You make it with your seed, your faith and by following God's wisdom for your life (Matthew 6:33).

5. **Stop underestimating yourself.** God chose to live inside of you. You were born to get ahead.

6. **DARE TO ASK & THINK BIG!** Refuse to be stamped by your financial, educational or emotional limitations. There are no limits with God. We limit Him when we think small. Ephesians 3:20 says God's ability corresponds to what we DARE to ASK and DARE to THINK.

THINK IT & SAY IT

I embrace a mindset of abundance. I refuse to allow excuses to limit me and keep me stuck in my life, spiritually, emotionally or financially. I am the head and not the tail. What I am, on the inside, is where I'm going on the outside— I am getting ahead. My success is in my seed and I DARE to ask BIG and think BIG, in Jesus' Name!

Day 23
"I Can't Expect To Be Blessed All The Time."

Today we're fasting from the thought that says, "I can't expect to be blessed ALL the time." We have bought the lie that things can't be good all the time. Yet God says that goodness and mercy will follow us ALL the days of our lives. We have to eliminate expectations of failure and mediocrity.

LET'S CHANGE IT TODAY

1. **God HAS already blessed you in heavenly places** (Ephesians 1:3). So EXPECT those blessings to show up "ON EARTH as it is in heaven." Our words connect heaven's blessings to earth. As you speak God's promises, you activate His blessings.

2. **Jesus took ALL the curse so you could have ALL the blessing** (Galatians 3:13)! We must realize WHY we can be blessed all the time: because Jesus paid the price in His blood, for the blessing of God to be ours.

3. **Because you are IN CHRIST, you are BLESSED COMING IN AND BLESSED GOING OUT** (Deuteronomy 28:6). ...In the city & in the field... This speaks of continual blessing wherever you are and wherever you go.

4. **Don't try to follow the blessings.** The blessings are designed to follow you and overtake you in Christ (Deuteronomy 28:2, Galatians 3:13)!

5. **Forever forgiven = Forever blessed.** (Romans 4:7-8). God's kingdom is set up so that blessing follows the man or woman who knows they are forgiven. Knowing

you are forgiven by the blood of Jesus paves the way to your divine inheritance (Acts 26:17).

6. **You are magnetic! You attract whatever you believe about yourself. Believe that God HAS blessed you** (Genesis 12:1-3). Blessings are attracted to an attitude of EXPECTATION. SET YOUR EXPECTATION ON BEING BLESSED!

THINK IT & SAY IT

God has already blessed me. I cannot be cursed. In Christ, I have ALL the blessings of the Old and New Testament. I don't have to chase down the blessings. Goodness and mercy will follow me all the days of my life. The blessings of God will follow me, chase me down, and overtake me. I am forever forgiven, therefore I am forever blessed. I expect blessings all the time, in Jesus' Name.

Day 24
"I Can't Control My Emotions."

Today we're fasting from the thoughts that say: "I can't control my emotions. I'm such an emotional person. My emotions get the best of me."

We all have emotions, but unfortunately sometimes THEY have us!

God created us to live with positive and healthy emotions. It's the negative ones that can harm our lives, our relationships and our future. The idea that we are "victims" of our emotions because of our gender, our culture, our nationality, or our personality type, has to be eliminated.

LET'S CHANGE IT TODAY

1. **Our emotions are the result of our thoughts.** If you think sad thoughts, you will become sad. If you think joyful and happy thoughts, you will become happy. As a man thinks within, so is he (Proverbs 23:7).

2. **Reject the belief that your emotions are the result of your culture, race or gender.** Your culture may be more or less expressive of emotions, but we are all both spiritual and emotional beings.

3. **You have been given SELF-CONTROL.** It is in you. 2 Timothy 1:7 says, "God has given you power, love and a sound mind" (SELF-CONTROL). Galatians 5:23 says the fruit of the spirit includes SELF-CONTROL, and the spirit is in you!

4. **Believe you are in control.** As you control your thoughts, you will control your emotions. THEN, you will not feel the urge to control others!

5. **You can remember what happiness is.** Jeremiah FORGOT what happiness was, because he talked himself into misery (Lamentations 3:17). When he began to think about the goodness of God, JOY WAS RESTORED. Emotions follow thoughts—whether good or bad.

6. **Express your emotions UPWARD; and you won't need to always express them OUTWARD.** When you pour your heart and feelings out to God, the temptation to explode at others will be diminished.

THINK IT & SAY IT

I am not under the control of my emotions anymore. They are under my control. As I fill my mind with good thoughts, they will become good emotions. I can control my emotions by my thought life, and my thought life is surrendered to God's Word. I have self-control and dominion over my life. And from this day forward, my emotions serve me, rather than control me. I pour my emotions out to God, and I don't need to pour them out to others, in Jesus' Name!

Day 25

"Don't Get Your Hopes Up."

Today we're fasting from the thought that says: "Don't get your hopes up."

This mindset has subtly found its way into our heads. We have been trained by doubt and unbelief to lower our expectations—to brace ourselves for mediocrity and status quo.

To hope is to look up—to have expectation! To hope is to live. Hope is like oxygen. It's like light in a dark and negative world.

Proverbs 13:12 says: "Hope deferred makes the heart sick." There are many great truths from this Scripture.

When hope is "put off to the side," your heart becomes sick. When your hopes are "dashed to the ground", your heart becomes sick. Most importantly, your heart becomes sick when you STOP hoping. Hope HEALS!

LET'S CHANGE IT TODAY

1. **GET YOUR HOPES UP, no matter what.** Psalm 78:7 says, "that they might set their hope in God." Put your hope in our unfailing God, not people who disappoint.

2. **KEEP THEM UP.** I John 3:3 says to FIX your hope on Him, and it will purify you. To fix means: to remain, to attach, to be glued. Glue your hopes on God. He will not disappoint.

3. **It's ok when you don't see what you're hoping for.** The fact that you don't see it gives hope a reason to

remain alive in your heart. Once you have something and see it, you don't need to hope for it anymore. It's when you don't see it, that your hope has a reason to exist.

4. **Get Faith.** Faith is a tangible force. It is a substance. If you are exercising faith, no one will be able to tell you that God's promise will not come to pass. Faith gives substance to what you are hoping for. Hope comes from the encouragement in Scripture (Romans 15:4). And faith comes from hearing God's Word (Romans 10:17). As you exercise faith by believing what God says, you overcome opposition and faith helps bring to pass what you are hoping for.

5. **Meditate on the love of God.** Hope that <u>IS NOT DEFERRED</u> (delayed, or disappointed) comes from love. Romans 5:5 says, "...and hope does not disappoint (or leave you with shame), because the love of God has been shed abroad in your heart." Love is the FORCE that eliminates disappointment when you are hoping for something. Keep your mind fixed on God's love for you.

6. **Fire the "management" team.** Free yourself from people who think they're doing you a favor by "managing" your expectations, or "protecting" you from disappointment. Get around "hopers" and dreamers and people who are filled with expectation! It's ok if people want to help DEFINE your hopes; but NEVER let them CONFINE your hopes.

THINK IT & SAY IT

My hopes are up! I eliminate the notion of lowering my expectations. I refuse to accept people's advice to "not get my hopes up." I get my hopes up NOW and I keep them up. I expect God's promises to come to pass in my life today! I expect good to come to my life today, in my family, in my home, in my church, in my job, in my relationships, in my body, and in my finances. I expect ideas, favor, and wisdom. I look up, expecting to receive the best of what God has for me today. Faith and love are keeping my hope alive and will protect me from disappointment. I have unlimited and unhindered hope and expectation in Jesus' Name.

Day 26
"Something Bad Is Going To Happen To Me."

Today, we're fasting from the thought that says, "Something bad is going to happen to me." Fear is sometimes defined as "False Expectations Appearing Real." We must cast down the thoughts that create negative and false expectations. Often, when things are going good, we start embracing ourselves for something to go bad.

LET'S CHANGE IT TODAY

1. **Remember, expectation is the womb of manifestation** (Acts 3:5). Lets look up to God, with expectation that we are going to receive something good today. Every good gift comes from above, from your Heavenly Father (James 1:17). Expect!

2. **Believe God's promise.** In Psalm 91:10 the Message translation, it says, "Evil can't get close to you. Harm can't get through the door. He ordered His angels to guard you wherever you go." YES! Believe TODAY that harm can't get through the door. No evil is coming to you!

3. **Give God something to work with.** Ephesians 3:20 says He is able to do exceeding abundantly beyond all that we can ask or think. So ask big & think big.

4. **Ask for good to come your way.** In the same way that we HAVE NOT because we ask not, we also can HAVE, because we do ask (James 4:2).

5. **Don't just wake up expecting. Go to bed expecting!** Psalm127:2 says God gives to His beloved WHILE

they are sleeping. Believe that BECAUSE you are His beloved, He loves you, He will give good things to you while you are sleeping. Go to sleep expecting!

6. **Love God** (Romans 8:28). Even bad things that happen around you will TURN INTO GOOD for those who love God and are called according to His purpose. That's YOU! The antidote to anything bad happening in your life, is love. Love God and watch things turn around for good!

THINK IT & SAY IT

I look up today expecting to receive good in my life from God. Every good gift comes from Him. My eyes are on Him. Even the bad things that have happened in my life are turning around for good. I wake up expecting good to come my way, and I go to bed expecting good to come my way. He gives to me even in my sleep! Something good is going to happen to me today, in Jesus' Name!

Day 27
"I'm Inferior."

Today we're fasting from the thought that says, "I'm inferior."

Ever felt like that? Or inferiority's offspring: "I don't measure up"; "I feel small"; "I feel insignificant," etc. It's time to get rid of this thinking.

LET'S CHANGE IT TODAY

1. **Take a look at the new seating chart** (Ephesians 2:6)! You don't have to MEASURE up, because God has RAISED you up and seated you with Him! You are in authority and have power over the circumstances and challenges of this life.

2. **Stop beating yourself up.** You are approved by God TODAY (Mark 1:11). You are accepted in the beloved (Ephesians 1:7). Believe it.

3. **See yourself above only and not beneath** (Deuteronomy 28:13). You are the head and not the tail. Remember, what you SEE is what will BE.

4. **See yourself BIG today.** Replace the grasshopper image with the image of a giant. 1 John 4:4 says, "GREATER is He that is in you..." God is bigger than any mountain or problem and He lives in you. For Him to fit INSIDE of you makes you pretty huge (in the spirit)!

5. **You have what it takes.** You have the mind of Christ (1 Corinthians 2:16). and you have a treasure in you: the ability to call light out of darkness (2 Corinthians 4:6). The devil wants you to think that others have what it takes to win, but you don't. That's a lie. Reject this lie with the truth of who you are.

6. Remember: Royalty Destroys Inferiority. Acquaint yourself with your new bloodline. You are royalty in Christ. This makes you reign over life. Believe it (Romans 5:17). When you know that you are made righteous and made royal by His blood, it makes you BOLD AS A LION (Proverbs 28:1)!

THINK IT & SAY IT

I am seated with Jesus Christ in heavenly places. I am above only and not beneath. I am approved by God. I have what it takes. God has put a treasure in me and equipped me with the Holy Spirit and power to be up to any task, I am not inferior to anyone or anything. I have the royal blood of Jesus running through my veins. I am His righteousness, and therefore, I am as bold as a lion, reigning in this life in Jesus' Name!

Day 28
"I'm Running Out."

Today we're fasting from the thought that says, "I'm running out."

This is a mindset that we WILL overcome today. The thought that you're running out of time; running out of money; running out of patience, strength, chances, etc. This thinking has to go!

LET'S CHANGE IT TODAY

1. **Replace 'running-out' thinking with 'running-OVER' thinking** (Psalm 23:5). Expect your cup to run over TODAY. Your cup is your container. And in Christ, God keeps pouring blessing into your life, so your container can't hold it all in!

2. **Know His Name!** El Shaddai = The God of MORE THAN ENOUGH! God's name represents His character and His nature. He IS more than enough, so HE GIVES more than enough. You could NEVER exhaust the infinite riches and supply of God (Genesis 17:1-2, Genesis 28:3).

3. **HE RENEWS** (Isaiah 40:31), **HE RESTORES** (JOEL 2:25), **HE RECOVERS** (1 Samuel 30:8), and **HE RUNS** you over with blessing (Deuteronomy 28:2).

4. **Remember Elijah and the widow NEVER ran out.** The jar of flour will never be empty and the jar of oil will never run dry (1 Kings 17:14). If they never ran out, **YOU will never run out** (Acts 10:34-35).

5. **Think like a giver.** You never RUN OUT of what you give away. It always comes back: good measure, pressed down, shaken together and RUNNING OVER (Luke 6:38, Matthew 14:20)!

6. **Plan on what you're going to do with all your extra time, money, and opportunities.** YES—God will give you MORE than you can contain, which keeps you giving it away (Malachi 3:10)!

THINK IT & SAY IT

I embrace a "running over" mentality. I set my expectation on being run over with God's blessing. My cup, my money, my time, and my chances are POURING over in my life. God did it for the widow, He will do it for me. He is MY GOD—the God of more than enough, and I expect it today. I think like a giver and I know that whatever I give away will always come back to me in good measure, pressed down, shaken together and RUNNING OVER, in Jesus' Name.

Day 29
"God Is Far From Me."

Today, let's fast from the thought that says: "God is far from me."

The serpent was subtle in Genesis 3. Thoughts that can defeat us are often very subtle thoughts too.

We have to learn to not only discern between right and wrong; but we must discern between "right" and "almost right."

It's "almost right" to ask God to come down and help us. It sounds holy. It sounds humble. But you will truly be free when you discover, HE IS ALREADY HERE. Emmanuel means "God with us." When Jesus came to the earth, He put an end to the separation between God and man.

Not only is God with us. Not only is God for us. But He is also IN US.

This is an amazing mystery, and we won't understand it completely until we are in heaven. Colossians 1:27 says "...this mystery, which is Christ in you, the hope of glory." It's "almost right" to believe that if we become holier, we can get closer to God.

But the separation between us and God is a myth. It's an illusion. The devil wants us to believe it to keep us powerless and misinformed concerning our connection with God. It's true that in Isaiah 59:2 it says that "your sins have made a separation between you and your God." But Jesus TOOK AWAY the sin through His blood. Therefore, THERE IS NO SEPARATION between us and God anymore, if we have been born-again. It's our failure to recognize this that keeps us in bondage, feeling distant from God. We feel sometimes, He is so far away. But He is not. He is here. He is there.

LET'S CHANGE IT TODAY

1. **Psalm 46:1 says, "He is an ever-PRESENT help in times of trouble."** WOW! You have to love this thought. Have you ever had times of trouble? But notice, He is ever-present. THEN, it says, "help" in times of trouble. **It is His "ever-presence" that brings us help in times of trouble.**

2. **Take Him at His Word.** Jesus said in Matthew 28:20, "Lo, I am with you always; even to the end of the age." There is no way to misinterpret this verse. "I am with you always." That has to warm your heart and comfort you.

3. **Christianity is not a life of attainment, but a life of recognition.** Philemon 6 says, "that your faith might become effective, through the acknowledgement of those things which are already in you, in Christ Jesus." Many people focus on "attaining" God's presence and God's blessing. But the Scripture is clear that we must recognize and acknowledge that He is already in us. His gifts are already in us. This produces power that MONEY and RELIGION cannot buy! The first part of the verse says this is what makes your faith become effective. Acknowledge. Recognize. He is already in you. His gifts are in you.

4. **Christianity is not us "finding God."** It's that He came and found us, spilled His blood to cleanse us from all unrighteousness, took us into His arms, and breathed His very Spirit into us. Now He lives in every person that has accepted Jesus Christ as their Lord. Romans 8:11 says, "and if the same Spirit that raised Jesus from the dead, lives in you, then He who raised up Christ Jesus from the dead, will give life to your mortal bodies through His Spirit that indwells in you."

5. **Eliminate every thought that says, "God, come down and help me" or "Send your Spirit."** He has already come. He has already sent His Spirit. Our battle is to believe this whether we feel His presence or not. He is in us!

6. **It's not us living FOR God. It's us LIVING FROM GOD.** Galatians 2:20 says, "It is no longer I who lives, but Christ lives in me." David said in Psalm 139:7-9, "Where can I go from Your Spirit? Where can I flee from Your presence? If I go to heaven You are there. If I make my bed in Sheol, You are there. If I take the wings of the dawn and dwell in the uttermost parts of the sea, even THERE Your hand will lead me, and Your right hand will hold me."

THINK IT & SAY IT

I decide today to eliminate the thought that I am separated from God in any way. He is an ever-present help in my time of trouble. His ever-presence brings me help! And I will rest in knowing I am in His presence.

I recognize that He is already in me. That's what makes my faith work. He has found me and put His Spirit in me. The very same Spirit that raised Jesus from the dead is living on the inside of me.

God is not far off. He is right here, right now. I am surrounded by His love and enveloped in His presence. Therefore I am not afraid.

He is my shield and refuge. My fortress and my very present help today. I am not trying to live FOR God; I am living FROM Him. His power is in me. His presence is in me. His love is in me. And nothing can ever separate me from the love of God which is in Christ Jesus my Lord!

Day 30
"The Battle Is So Hard."

Today we are fasting from the thought: "The battle is so hard."

Perhaps you're battling depression, an addiction, or fear. Perhaps it's a sickness or pain. Regardless of what it is, you're going to receive the victory today! We need to take this thought captive which says, "the battle is so hard."

LET'S CHANGE IT TODAY

1. **YOU'VE ALREADY WON!** Jesus' declaration on the cross sums it up: "It is finished" (John 19:30). What was finished? The battle against the power of sin and the devil was finished. The fulfillment of the law was finished. The price for us to be saved and made victorious was PAID IN FULL!

2. **Ask God to open the eyes of your heart** (Ephesians 1:18-19). You must look at life from God's point of view. In 2 Kings 6, when Elisha was surrounded by enemy armies, his servant became afraid and said, 'we're surrounded, what should we do?' Elisha didn't pray for more angels. He prayed: "Lord, open the eyes of my servant that he would see there are more for us than those against us" (2 Kings 6:17). Suddenly, he saw chariots of fire and a host of angels surrounding their enemies! The battle was already won.

3. **Believe you have it!** In Mark 11:24, Jesus said, "That's why I tell you to have faith that you have already received whatever you pray for, and it will be yours." That's power this world can't give you and money can't buy! Remember 1 Peter 2:24 "...with His stripes you WERE healed." Notice, God speaks to us in past tense. It's already yours!

4. **ONLY BELIEVE.** Stick to what God said! John 6:29 says, "This is our work: TO BELIEVE." In other words, BEFORE you pray for rain, bring your umbrella! Expect it to happen. Remember, it's "the good fight of faith" (1 Timothy 6:12). Our job is to believe. Our battle is to believe what God has done and what is already ours. 2 Chronicles 20:15 says the battle is not yours, but God's.

5. **Praise God that you HAVE the victory.** In 2 Chronicles 20:22 it says, "As they began to sing and praise the Lord, the Lord sent ambushes and their enemies were defeated."

THINK IT & SAY IT

I already have the victory in my life. Jesus has already won my battles for me. My fight is to believe. I refuse to stop believing. I walk by faith and not by sight. I'm the head and not the tail. There are ALREADY more for me than those against me.

I cast my care and trouble on God. He is fighting for me. He is interceding for me right now! I rejoice in the midst of my battles, no matter what things look like. I choose to praise God, in Jesus' Name.

Day 31
"WHATEVER HAPPENS MUST BE GOD'S WILL."

Do you realize that your life is changing for the better, just as the Bible said it would? We are being TRANSFORMED by the renewing of our minds, and we are coming into the perfect will of God.

Many times our minds (and the devil) tells us that if things don't go our way that must be God's will. That's wrong thinking!

Today we are fasting from the thought that says: "God must not want me to have this." Or "Whatever happens must be God's will."

Please note, I realize many of us reading this know theologically that God's will is for good. But in our lives, when we face resistance or it seems like God is not responding, we're tempted to give up and accept whatever happens as God's will.

LET'S CHANGE IT TODAY

If there ever was a story that best illustrates how to change this mindset, it is the story of blind Bartimaeus. When he heard Jesus had the power to heal, he began to cry out, "Jesus, have mercy on me" (Mark 10:46-52)! Many people told him to be quiet, but he cried out even more. He refused to accept this condition as God's will. Neither should we!

1. **Stop listening to voices trying to keep you the way you are. There are voices in your head saying, "Keep quiet."** There are voices from others saying, "Stay the way you are." There are voices saying, "God must not

want you to have this." NO. NO. NO. NO. NO. Say "no" to those voices and keep going after whatever you see in God's Word.

2. **When you face resistance, add persistence!** In verse 48, when people tried to shut Bartimaeus up, he cried out even more. Press through until you receive your promise!

3. **Don't give up.** When Jesus heard Bartimeaus crying out, He stood still. Don't give up or move away until you have Jesus' attention. When your persistence causes Jesus to stop and notice you, your miracle is on its way!

4. **Believe God wants to fulfill your desires, not just your needs.** In verse 51, Jesus said, "What do you want Me to do for you?" Truthfully, Bartimaeus could have lived without sight, but Jesus asked him what he wanted, not just what he needed. God doesn't just meet our needs. He fulfills our desires – provided that our desires are founded on Scriptural promises (Psalm 37:4).

5. **Make up your mind that you will not be denied.** Bartimaeus would not be denied. The woman with the issue of blood would not be denied. The mother of the demon-possessed daughter would not be denied (Mark 5:25-34, Matt. 15:22-28). You and I will not be denied.

THINK IT & SAY IT

I decide today that I will stop listening to the voices in my head and around me that are telling me to stay the way I am.

I will not be quiet when I face resistance. My prayers will not be silenced by doubt, fear or opposition.

At times when I may feel God is not answering, I will stick to His Word. God says "Yes" to what He has already promised;

therefore, I will stand on His promises in all areas of my life. And I will not be denied.

I believe that God wants to give me the desires of my heart, and not just my needs. When I face resistance, I will add persistence.

I will not give up or give in to my present condition. I will press through the opposition and not be denied. I will not tolerate a present condition of discouragement, sickness, poverty or mediocrity—<u>NOT ANOTHER DAY OF MY LIFE.</u>

Psalm 37:4 says, "He will give me the desires of my heart." I will keep thinking this, believing this, and expecting this until something changes for my good, in Jesus' Name!

Day 32
"God Is Mad At Me."

Today, we are fasting from the thought that says, "God is mad at me."

Many people think that God is mad at them, or the reason bad things are happening is because God is against me. Or, perhaps you don't think He's overtly against you, but He's just not aggressively helping you.

Wrong thoughts are designed by the devil and our flesh to undermine our faith. If you think God is mad at you, you won't be expectant toward God to bless you.

Let's take this thought captive (the word "captive" means: "to conquer with a sword." We conquer wrong thinking with the sword of God's word!)

LET'S CHANGE IT TODAY

1. **God is not mad AT you. He is mad ABOUT you!** This is something I started saying many years ago when I discovered God's love. And I will never stop believing it! When you accept this thought, you will have confidence, expectation and peace. Who couldn't use that! How do I know this is true? Romans 8:38-39 says "Nothing can separate you from the love of God..." You are forgiven (1 John 1:9) and you are LOVED (1 John 4:10).

2. **Think this new thought: God loves me as much as He loves Jesus!** In John 17:23 Jesus says to the Father: "I in them and You in Me, that they may be perfected in unity, that the world may know that You sent Me, and LOVED THEM, AS MUCH AS YOU HAVE LOVED ME!" What an amazing truth. God loves you as much as He loves Jesus. And there is no way God can be mad at Jesus.

3. **He thinks precious thoughts about you ALL THE TIME!** Psalm 139:17-18 says, "How precious are Your thoughts toward me, O God...If I should count them, they would outnumber the sand. When I awake, I am still with you!"

4. **What God said to Jesus, is the SAME to you: "You are My beloved Son. In You, I am well-pleased"** (Mark 1:11). Hallelujah! He doesn't sound mad at Jesus! He sounds "mad about Him!" Well, 1 John 4:16 says, "As He is, so are we." Look, there is no getting around this marvelous truth: God doesn't love Jesus half-heartedly, therefore He doesn't love you half-heartedly either.

5. **There is nothing God is holding back from you!** Romans 8:32 says "He who did not spare His own Son, but delivered Him up for us all, how shall He not also with Him, freely give us all things!"

6. **YOU ARE NOT CONDEMNED!** Romans 8:1 says, "There is no condemnation for those who are in Christ Jesus..." Condemnation is an expression of strong disapproval. God approves of you, because of your faith in Jesus, not because you have done everything right. God's love for you is non-negotiable. Jeremiah 31:3 says He loves you with an everlasting love. It cannot be stopped, quenched or compromised.

THINK IT & SAY IT

God is not mad at me, He is mad about me. He loves me as much as Jesus. He thinks precious thoughts about me all the time! I am His beloved, and He is mine!

There is nothing God is holding back from me. He didn't hold back His best, therefore He won't hold back the rest!

I refuse to be condemned. I am forgiven. I reject the thought that He is mad at me or against me. God is for me, and not against me. His love toward me cannot be stopped, quenched or compromised, in Jesus' Name.

Day 33
"If I Can Just Stop Sinning, I'll Be Holy And Pleasing To God."

Today we're fasting from the thought that says, "If I can just stop sinning, I'll be holy and pleasing to God."

While its obviously better not to sin, the thinking that holiness is obtained by our sinlessness is wrong thinking.

LET'S CHANGE IT TODAY

1. **Re-define the correct meaning of 'holiness'.** Holy doesn't mean 'detaching' from all that is bad. It means 'attaching' to the LOVE of GOD.

2. **Remember Adam & Eve.** As long as they fellowshipped with God in the garden, they didn't sin. It was only when they separated themselves that temptation had its power (Genesis 3:1-8).

3. **Expect to taste God's goodness** (Psalm 34:8). Once you drink from the cup of His goodness, you'll no longer hold your cup up to the bitter fancies of sin. When you drink the best, you don't want to taste the rest!

4. **Reverse this thinking.** When you are pleasing to God, sin loses its power. And God is pleased by your faith (Hebrews 11:6).

5. **Be BELIEVING!** The sin that leads to other sins is the sin of "not believing what God says or what God has done" (John 16:9). When you believe Him, you please Him, even with your flaws.

6. **Accept the gift of righteousness.** When you awake to righteousness, it produces power over sin (1 Corinthians 15:34). We've had it backwards, thinking that when we stop sinning, we will be righteous. But the truth is, when we realize how we have been made righteous in Christ, we are empowered to turn from sin.

THINK IT & SAY IT

I attach myself to the love of God, and therefore I am walking in true holiness. Attachment to Him repels sin and temptation from me. I expect to taste God's goodness and lose my appetite for sin. I believe what God has done and what He says, and that is holy & pleasing to Him. I am the righteousness of God through the blood of Jesus! My heart awakens each day to the love, grace & righteousness of God. I am walking in God's power, and I am free from sin's power, in Jesus' Name!

Day 34
"I JUST CAN'T FORGIVE MYSELF."

Today we are fasting from the thought that says: "I just can't forgive myself."

Who hasn't thought that at one time or another? The devil would love to keep us in self-condemnation for the things we have done or failed to do. He knows it paralyzes us and prevents us from making the kind of impact that God intended for us.

I read of a young teenager who accidentally struck his 5 year old sister with a car, tragically killing her in their driveway. And as tragic as it is for a child to die in that way at such a young age, an even greater tragedy is the difficulty this young man will have forgiving himself. Though few of us have faced something as dramatic as this, we all need to overcome the thoughts that try to accuse us for what we have done.

LET'S CHANGE IT TODAY

1. **Realize that we only deserve forgiveness because of the blood of Jesus.** Not because what we did wrong "never happened," or it wasn't that bad. Give up rationalizations and excuses.

2. **It was that bad, but God is even MORE good!** James 2:13 says mercy triumphs over judgment. His mercy toward you TRUMPS your judgment over yourself. Believe that God is bigger than what you did. In Luke 22:34, Peter denied the Lord 3 times, and Jesus forgave him. Later, Peter preached the first sermon after Jesus rose from the dead, and 3000 people were saved in a

day! Peter was able to forgive himself when he knew Jesus had accepted him. In the same way, realize that you have been accepted by God, no matter what you have done—simply by believing in the work of the cross of Jesus Christ.

3. **Give up your right to hold against yourself ANYTHING that God Himself does not hold against you.** If God can forgive you, you can forgive yourself. His standard is absolute perfection, and He forgives you. Psalm 103:12 says, "As far as east is from west, so far has He removed our transgressions from us."

4. **Stop rehearsing what you did.** It's done. It's over. Now accept the second chance that God offers. Philippians 3:10 says "forgetting what lies behind, and reaching forward..." Reaching forward starts with thinking forward.

5. **Believe that guilt doesn't come from God.** He doesn't impose guilt on you to try to get you to stop doing something. Romans 2:4 says it is His lovingkindness that draws us to repentance. Since this guilt and shame doesn't come from God, there can be only one other source—the devil. James 4:7 says, "Submit to God——resist the devil——and he will flee from you."

6. **Give up the SELF-PUNISHMENT.** Some people have said to themselves: "I'll make myself feel bad to pay for what has been done." Why should we pay the price that has ALREADY been paid for what we've done wrong? Stop beating yourself up—no one beats us up better than ourselves. The fact is, whatever we have done that we can't seem to forgive ourselves for, is already forgiven. By trying to "pay for what we have done," we are insulting the very blood of Jesus that HAS PAID the price in full. Accept His free gift (Ephesians 1:7).

THINK IT & SAY IT

I receive mercy today, because of the blood of Jesus. Though I didn't deserve it, God proclaims over me, that I am "not guilty." Where I have failed, God's mercy triumphs over judgment.

I give up my right today to hold ANYTHING against myself. I deserve to be punished, but Jesus took THAT punishment for me. I forget what lies behind and press on, moving forward in my life with God, even though I feel like I have blown it beyond repair.

I reject this guilt and self-condemnation that the devil is trying to put on me. God is the God of second chances. I will no longer try to make myself feel bad to pay for what has been done. The price for what I did or failed at has been paid in full by God, in Jesus' Name!

Day 35
"I'M SO DEPRESSED."

Today we're fasting from the thought that says, "I'm so depressed." So often, depression is anger turned inward at ourselves for our shortcomings and mistakes.

Perhaps you've thought: "Life's a drag; what's the point of anything; I'll never be happy." These thoughts are designed to rob you of the joy and confidence that produce supernatural strength in our lives.

LET'S CHANGE IT TODAY

1. **Stop condemning yourself.** Condemnation is a mindset that robs you of joy and peace. Romans 14:22 says, "Happy is the man who does not condemn himself..." Don't condemn yourself because God doesn't condemn you.

2. **God's still working on you!** Philippians 1:6 says lighten up on yourself. He began a good work in you; He'll finish it! Trust God that you're making progress. You're not standing still.

3. **Tap into the power of believing.** 1 Peter 1:8 says: "...though you do not see Him now, you BELIEVE in Him, and are filled with inexpressible and glorious joy." Believe the promise of God regardless of what you see, and depression will begin to leave.

4. **Recognize and eliminate negative thoughts, one at a time.** For example, if you think, "This will never work," replace it immediately with, "It will work, because God is perfecting (completing) whatever concerns me" (Psalm 138:8).

5. **Surround yourself with positive people.** Positive thinking and speaking is contagious, just as negative thinking is. Surround yourself only with those who create an atmosphere of victory with their attitude words.

6. **Remember, you are not helpless.** Thoughts of helplessness bring depression. The Holy Spirit is our Helper (John 14:16-18; John 15:26; John 16:7). He has not left you alone and He will never leave you alone.

THINK IT & SAY IT

I will never be depressed another day in my life. I decide to stop condemning myself and beating myself up for my shortcomings. I believe God is working in me every day.

I am not a negative thinker. I am positive. God is for me, with me and in me, therefore depression cannot stay. I am not helpless because I have the Holy Spirit living in me. I command every ounce of depression to loose me and let me go. I command it to be removed and cast into the sea, in Jesus' Name!

Day 36
"If I Find The Right Person, Then I'll Be Happy."

Today, we're fasting from the thought that says, "If I just find the right person, I'll be happy." Or "If this person changes, I'll be happy."

LET'S CHANGE IT TODAY

1. **Refuse to accept that anyone has the power to make you happy.** When we depend on someone else to make us happy, we give them control of our emotions. We must take control of our own emotions (Genesis 4:6-7).

2. **Right relationships can make us happ-IER, but not happy.** Surround yourself with the right people, to strengthen your life, but not as the source of your life (Acts 2:42). Put your trust in God (Psalm 43:5).

3. **Stop trying to find the right person, and simply be the right person.** No matter who comes and goes from your life, you will always have to live with yourself. Learn to be happy with yourself by celebrating your strengths. Don't live in denial or fear of your weaknesses. Learn to strengthen them.

4. **Stop seeing yourself as incomplete.** You are complete in Christ (Colossians 1:28). No one else can complete you. They can complement you, but you don't depend on them to fulfill or complete you.

5. **Ask God for understanding today.** Understanding produces happiness (Proverbs 3:13).
6. **Give up comparing your life to anyone** (2 Corinthians 10:12). When we compare, we are WITHOUT understanding, and thus, without happiness.
7. **Happiness and joy come from meditating on the Words of Jesus** (John 15:11). Occupy your mind with Jesus' words. Your heart will be lifted to another level.

THINK IT & SAY IT

I refuse to depend on someone to make me happy. I take control of my emotions and I walk in divine happiness. My trust is in God. He completes me. Since I am in Christ, I receive supernatural understanding. I see myself, others and life from God's point of view. I will not compare, therefore I will not despair. I meditate on Jesus' words, and find true joy, in Jesus' Name.

Day 37
"How Could I Ever Recover From This Loss?"

Today we're fasting from the thought that says: "How could I ever recover from this loss?"

We've all lost something at one time or another in our lives. If it hasn't been money, it's been time or relationships, opportunity or HOPE. Well today, we begin to GET IT BACK!

We must abstain from the thought that "we can't recover," "we'll never know great days like we did in the past," or "I've lost too much to recover."

LET'S CHANGE IT TODAY

1. **Let this thought permeate your mind: God is a God of restoration.** Joel 2:25-26 says, "I will the restore the years that have been lost." Whether it's the stock market, bad decisions, what others have done to you—God will restore.

2. **Get rid of the mentality of "settling."** We must refuse to settle. The ten lepers wouldn't settle for their leprosy (Luke 17:11-19). They cried out to Jesus. The woman with the demon-possessed daughter wouldn't settle with her daughter's condition (Matthew 15:22). Bartimaeus wouldn't settle with blindness. He wouldn't stop until he recovered his sight (Mark 10:52). REFUSE to settle for the way things are.

3. **Realize God WANTS you to go to Him, and ask Him to avenge you.** In Luke 18, the unjust judge avenged the widow because of her persistence. HOW MUCH MORE will our just and loving God avenge His children (Luke 18:6-7)!

4. **All the promises of God are YES** (2 Corinthians 1:20). He has promised restoration and recovery—so ask Him for it TODAY. God wants you to recover more than you do. Believe this.

5. **Believe the promise: the thief has to repay 7-fold of what he's stolen** (Proverbs 6:31). The thief = the devil, time, the economy, fear. These are all thieves that you can expect to give back supernaturally what has been lost in your life.

6. **Re-position your thinking for expectation.** 90% of profits in the world made between 1980 and 2000 went to 1.5 % of the people. That means 98.5% weren't expecting much! Start expecting.

7. **Expect recovery!** "You shall surely overtake your enemies and you shall recover all" (1 Samuel 30:8). Restoration and the recovery of what has been lost in our lives is a divine promise. Stand on it today.

THINK IT & SAY IT

I will recover all that has been lost in my life. I expect the restoration of lost relationships, lost money, lost hope and lost opportunities. I will not settle for loss and lack. God will avenge me. He will restore what has been stolen from me. I ask Him and expect Him to avenge me of all that has been lost in my life. I call forth a seven-fold return of what has been taken from me, In Jesus' Name!

Day 38
"Will God Do It?"

Today we're fasting from the thought that says, "Will God do it?"

So often, we question whether God will answer our prayer, whether He will heal, or whether He will deliver or rescue us. We need to put an end to this thinking that blocks our faith and blocks God's power.

LET'S CHANGE IT TODAY

1. **Always start thinking about anything with A PROMISE FROM GOD'S WORD:** Psalm 37:5—"Commit your way to the Lord; trust also in Him, and He will bring it to pass." Be promise minded. He is watching over His promises to bring them to pass (Jeremiah 1:12).

2. **Think His way, and do things His way** (Psalm 37:5). Commit to thinking His thoughts and following His system—His way of doing things (i.e. sowing/reaping; forgiving; love; faith; trust, etc.).

3. **Know He has called you.** You may not be "called" to be a minister, but you are "called" to receive God's promises and purpose for your life! (1 Thessalonians 5:24 - The one who CALLED you is FAITHFUL, and HE WILL DO IT!)

4. **Turn your concerns over to Him.** Psalm 138:8 says, "He will accomplish (fulfill) what concerns me."

5. **Be convinced He does what He promises to do.** Isaiah 46:11 says, "...yea, I have spoken it, I will also bring it to pass..." 1 Kings 8:56 says that not one of His promises have failed.

6. **THINK possibility!** In Mark 9:23, Jesus said, "All things are possible to those who believe." Remember, you didn't make the promise. God did. That was His part. Your part is to simply believe.

7. **It's already DONE.** Meditate on the last three words Jesus spoke before He died: IT IS FINISHED (John 19:30)! His death established God's covenant of promise to you. It's done. Believe it.

THINK IT & SAY IT

I declare my God is faithful to do what He promised in my life. He will fulfill His promises which include saving, healing, restoring and blessing me. He is the same yesterday, today and forever. Jesus did it all on the cross. It is FINISHED. He has already provided for my every need. He will accomplish the things that concern me. He is watching over His promises to perform them. He has done it before and He will do it again, in Jesus' Name.

Day 39
"I CAN'T GET THE VICTORY."

Today we are fasting from the thought that says, "I can't get the victory!"

Sometimes our biggest problem is trying to obtain something we already have. We've all laughed at a dog chasing his own tail, never catching up to it, because it's already a part of him. That's what it's like when we don't renew our mind to the victory that is already ours. We are missing out on so much, because of the thought that we can't get the victory.

LET'S CHANGE IT TODAY

1. **You've already won.** The victory is yours NOW. You are NOW more than a conqueror (Romans 8:37)!

2. **IT IS FINISHED!** (John 19:30) Jesus' death on the cross settled your victory. You never have to be defeated another day in your life.

3. **Stop fighting the wrong fight.** Our fight is the fight of faith (1 Timothy 6:12). That's all we need to be fighting—to believe what God says. The struggle, the battle, the wrestling IS to HOLD ON to what the Scripture says!

4. **Expect to win every battle.** Thanks be to God who ALWAYS leads us in His triumph (2 Corinthians 2:14).

5. **You can't fail because LOVE NEVER FAILS** (1 Corinthians 13:8)! Stay hidden in God's love, and you will not fail.

6. Expect a turnaround in every apparent defeat (Romans 8:28). Even if you've failed—you've won, because Jesus' paid for your turnaround. And its only a matter of time before victory shows up in your life. Expect it.

THINK IT & SAY IT

I already have the victory! Jesus said, "it is finished." My battle has been won over sin, sickness, Satan, lack, fear, discouragement and all other things. IT IS FINISHED! I can't fail today, because the LOVE OF GOD IS IN ME, and love never fails. I will never be defeated another day in my life, in Jesus' Name!

Day 40
"It's Impossible."

As we come to the close of our 40 Day Fast from Wrong Thinking, we need to take the limits off of our thinking. In order to do so, we must abandon the thought that says: "It's IMPOSSIBLE."

Jesus said "All things are possible to him who believes" (Mark 9:23)!

What is in your life today that you have given up on or considered impossible? Whatever it is (provided it's legal!), don't ever give up. NEVER NEVER NEVER give up!

One Easter weekend, a major story broke in America, and the New York Times interviewed me, and asked: "Since this story is so big, will you be speaking about it at church on Easter?" "It certainly is a big story," I responded. "But SOMEONE RISING FROM THE DEAD IS EVEN BIGGER!" They then asked what I would specifically say about it. I answered: "If a man can rise from the dead, anything is possible!"

This is why we can get rid of the wrong thinking that says, "It's impossible."

LET'S CHANGE IT TODAY

1. **Think about the resurrection every day!** This reveals the miraculous power of God to do anything! We tend to save these thoughts for Easter, but we need to think about the resurrection ALL THE TIME. It awakens hope, faith, and the possibilities of God.

2. **Eliminate thinking that says, "I can't believe that."** Cynicism and skepticism have filled our culture. We need to get out of the habit of questioning and

doubting the possibility of things. When you think there's no way, remember that JESUS IS THE WAY!

3. **Deal with the real problem.** It's not whether God will help. It's whether we believe. The man with the demon-possessed son came to Jesus and said, "If you can do anything, help us..." Jesus responded and said, "If you can believe..." See it's not whether God can do it. It's whether we can believe it. And remember that faith comes from hearing God's Word (Romans 10:17).

4. **You are bigger than a mountain! Believe that your words move mountains.** Matthew 17:20 says, "You shall say to this mountain, 'Remove from here to there', and it shall remove; and nothing shall be impossible to you." That's big!

5. **Meditate on people who had an impossible turnaround.** Abraham was 99 years old when he had a son. Sarah was 90! Moses parted the Red Sea. The list goes on and on. Find those people in the Bible and fill your mind with their testimonies. Hebrews 12:1 says, "We have a great cloud of witnesses surrounding us..." If it could happen for them, it can happen for you, and IT WILL.

6. **God CAN'T lie.** There is only ONE THING in this world that is impossible: its impossible for God to lie (Hebrews 6:18). Don't throw away your confidence in God's promises. He will fulfill them.

THINK IT & SAY IT

I will never be defeated another day in my life. I am redeemed from failure and defeat. I am the head and not the tail. Everything I put my hand to will succeed and prosper. No matter what is against me, I expect the tables to turn to my favor. My faith will not fail, because Jesus is praying for it! Amen!

Conclusion

Now that you've begun this THINKING FORWARD From the Inside Out, let me encourage you with a few final thoughts.

1. **Review regularly.** Don't let up. Life will try to pull you back into wrong thinking. Whenever a negative thought comes back, go back and review how to overcome this thought from that particular day.

2. **Share your testimony.** Something else that will keep you walking in victory is sharing how God has changed your life. Please send me your testimony at www.thinkingfast.org. This will encourage someone else to know that their life can be changed too!

3. **Help me take this revolution to the world.** God has called us to change the world, one life at a time, one thought at a time. You can help me take this revolutionary message to millions of others around the world by sowing a seed of change in others. Just log onto **www.thinkingfast.org** and click on "Make a Donation." Stand with me in getting the word out about this life-changing fast from wrong thinking.

4. **Finally, don't ever forget** there is no stopping the man or woman who is set free from wrong thinking. Remember, "As a man thinks within, so is he" (Proverbs 23:7)!